WHERE I LIVE

In a Village

Honor Head

WAYLAND

Explore the world with **Popcorn -** your complete first non-fiction library.

Look out for more titles in the Popcorn range. All books have the same format of simple text and striking images. Text is carefully matched to the pictures to help readers to identify and understand key vocabulary. www.waylandbooks.co.uk/popcorn

First published in 2010 by Wayland
Copyright © Wayland 2010

Wayland
Hachette Children's Books
338 Euston Road
London NW1 3BH

Wayland Australia
Level 17/207 Kent Street
Sydney NSW 2000

 Produced for Wayland by
White-Thomson Publishing Ltd
www.wtpub.co.uk
+44 (0)843 208 7460

Editor: Jean Coppendale
Designer: Clare Nicholas
Commissioned photography: Chris Fairclough
Picture Researcher: Amy Sparks
Series consultant: Kate Ruttle
Design concept: Paul Cherrill

With special thanks to Kira and her family and the people of
Hartington, in Derbyshire, for their help with this book.

British Library Cataloging in Publication Data
Honor Head
   In a Village - (Popcorn. Where I Live)
   1. Villages -- Great Britain -- Pictorial works -- Juvenile literature
   I. Title II. Series
   941.009734-dc22

ISBN: 978 0 7502 6316 0

Wayland is a division of Hachette Children's Books,
an Hachette UK company.
www.hachette.co.uk

Printed and bound in China

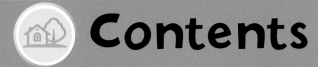 Contents

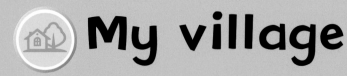

My village

My name is Kira. I live in a small village in the countryside. I live in a house called a cottage.

My cottage is built from local stone.

green fields

main road

paddock

general store

There is one main road that runs through the village. There are lots of small side roads.

A village is smaller than a town or city.

My village is in the middle of green fields and hills.

church

5

My school

I walk to school with my sister.
The school is in the next street.

There are three classrooms, two playgrounds and an adventure playground at school.

Near the school there is a nature reserve. Sometimes our teacher takes us there for a lesson. We learn the names of trees and birds.

What would you enjoy doing in the nature reserve?

No-one can build on a nature reserve so animals and plants are protected.

Nature Reserve

Derbyshire Wildlife Trust
Hartington Meadows

THE wildlife TRUSTS

Hartington Meadows Nature Reserve : a walk

This 2.5km (1 hour) circular walk takes you through the flower-rich pastures and hay meadows of the nature reserve to return to the car park on the Tissington Trail.

On your walk you can expect to see an abundance of flowers, including cowslips in the spring, delicate grasses such as the shimmering quaking grass, orchids in the summers and dropwort with its lacy white flowers. This is a real limestone speciality.

These areas are managed by Derbyshire Wildlife Trust working closely with local farmers. Please remember that grass is a valuable crop for farmers and keep to the marked paths. Note the intensively farmed and heavily fertilised fields around. With a more or less complete absence of wild flowers these fields are a stark comparison to those of the nature reserve.

Skylarks can usually be heard singing as they hang in the air - these farmland birds have declined dramatically in numbers in recent years. You may also hear the distinctive 'cronk-cronk' call of ravens that breed in nearby quarries. In spring you may also be lucky enough to see the exhibition of their aerial tumbling displays. In summer butterflies, grasshoppers and other insects should accompany you on most of the walk.

The disused sand pit is of geological interest. Sands and clays were extracted from here last century and used to make refractory bricks to line the kilns associated with the limestone quarries. These pocket deposits of sand and clay are about 6 million years old and formed in solution hollows in the underlying limestone which itself was formed over 300 million years ago when this area was covered in shallow tropical seas.

Derbyshire Wildlife Trust is the county's leading conservation organisation. We need your support to help us protect valuable sites like this for future generations.

Become a member - children can join Wildlife Watch, the wildlife club for young people

Volunteer with the Trust

Make a donation

For further details contact us at Derbyshire Wildlife Trust

www.derbyshirewildlifetrust.org.uk

Charity no 222213

Guidelines for visitors

Nature reserves are special places, providing protection for our precious wildlife. To help us keep them special, please observe the following guidelines when visiting this or our other reserves.

- To avoid disturbing plants or animals, please stay on the paths.
- Dogs disturb wildlife and livestock. Please keep them on a lead at all times.
- The collecting of flowers, plants or animals is not permitted and special care should be taken to avoid disturbing nesting birds.
- Please do not light fires or leave any litter.
- Grazes of 10 or more visitors should seek permission from the Trust's reserves staff before going on a reserve.

Please comply with the above and with the requests of a warden or any other Trust official.

Skylark

Common blue butterflies

Protecting Wildlife for the Future

Key
---- Public Footpath
.... Wildlife Walk
Concession Path
Shelter Belt
Reserve
Access by special permit only

Silica Sand Pit

Car Park

You are here

Tissington Trail

After school

After school I feed the ponies.

They live in a paddock in the village.

The ponies like to eat sugar cubes and pieces of carrot.

Sometimes we visit my granny.
She lives in a cottage down a lane.
The lane doesn't have a pavement
so we have to watch out for cars.

Along the lane there are hedgerows
where wild grass and flowers grow.

Village church

The village was built around the church. This is where many people go for church services.

The graveyard is where people are buried after they die.

graveyard

The village green is near the church.
This is a piece of grassy land. It has
a pond with ducks and geese.

I like to feed the ducks on the pond.

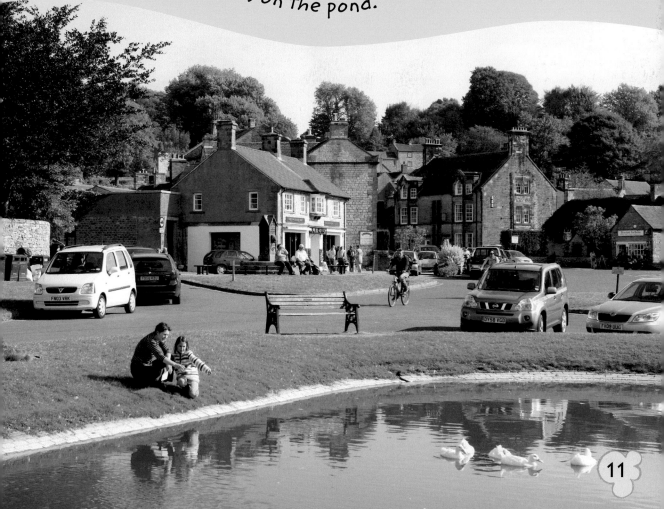

At the weekend

During the summer we ride our bicycles along the country lanes. We see farm animals in the fields.

We have lovely views across the fields and hills.

Sheep and cows like to eat the grass.

Sometimes we stop by the river.
There is a wooden bridge that
goes across the river.

Dad and I walk across the bridge to see
if we can spot any fish in the river.

At the farm

Sometimes we visit the farm just outside the village. The farmer has cows. Every day the farmer milks the cows using special machines.

There is a big gate to stop the cows going onto the road.

Milk from the cows is sent to a factory and put into cartons.

The farmer also has chickens
and turkeys that live in big sheds.
The farmer sells eggs from
the chickens.

Would you like to
keep chickens?

chickens

turkeys

 # Shopping

Near my house is a shop called the general store. It sells food, sweets, cakes, toys and clothes.

We always stop and have a chat with the shop assistant.

The post office is
where we buy stamps.
Mum and dad also pay
some bills here.

The post office has
a little tea room
where people
meet to talk.

Village shops

There is a shop that sells local food. This is food that has been grown or made by people who live in the village or nearby.

These eggs come from the farmer's chickens. What else can you see that is for sale in this shop?

The pottery is where the potter makes pots and bowls. He sells his pots in the shop at the front of his pottery.

Have you ever made pots from clay?

Getting around

There are no clothes shops or big supermarkets in my village. We drive or take the bus to the nearest town to do the weekly shopping.

There is only one bus every half an hour.

Many people have bicycles.
Cycling is the best way
to visit friends in other
villages close by.

Cyclists wear safety
helmets, gloves and
a bright jacket.

safety
helmet

bright
jacket

gloves

Who works where?

Can you remember who works where
in the village? Match the faces below
to the pictures opposite to find out.

a

b

c

d

1

2

3

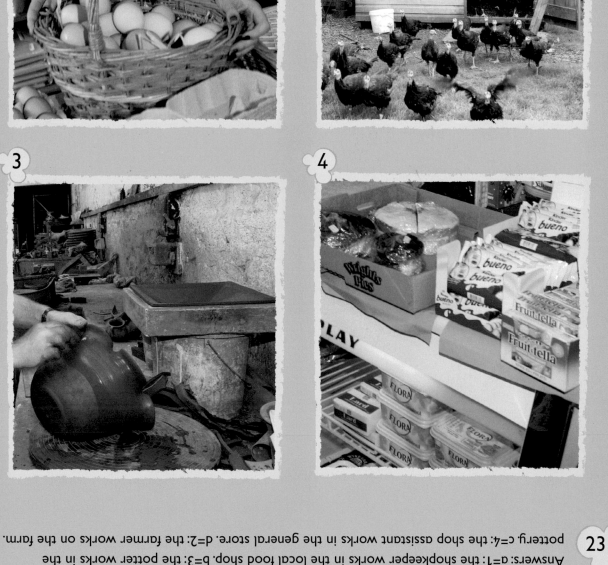

4

Answers: a=1: the shopkeeper works in the local food shop, b=3: the potter works in the pottery, c=4: the shop assistant works in the general store, d=2: the farmer works on the farm.

Glossary

bills money that has to be paid for things such as electricity, gas and water

church service when the priest leads a group in singing hymns and reading from the Bible

paddock an outdoor space where horses and ponies can eat grass

pottery a place where people make objects from clay

nature reserve an outdoor space that no-one can build on so that plants and animals can live there

Index

Where I Live

Contents of titles in the series:

WAYLAND